IMAGES
of America

PARKESBURG

This crowd has gathered in downtown Parkesburg on Main Street for the dedication of the World War I monument on July 4, 1924. (Gerald L. Treadway.)

On the cover: Parkesburg has always been a public-spirited community. This photograph shows a crowd gathering for the groundbreaking of a new fire station in 1934. (Parkesburg Free Public Library.)

IMAGES
of America

PARKESBURG

Bruce Edward Mowday
for the Parkesburg Free Library

ARCADIA
PUBLISHING

Published by Arcadia Publishing
Charleston SC, Chicago IL, Portsmouth NH, San Francisco CA

Library of Congress Control Number: 2009925586

For all general information contact Arcadia Publishing at:
Telephone 843-853-2070
Fax 843-853-0044
E-mail sales@arcadiapublishing.com
For customer service and orders:
Toll-Free 1-888-313-2665

Visit us on the Internet at www.arcadiapublishing.com

*Dedicated to those who have contributed to making Parkesburg
a wonderful place to work and live*

CONTENTS

ACKNOWLEDGMENTS

The leadership of the Parkesburg Free Library deserves credit for making this Arcadia book on the borough possible.

Library director Tom Knecht has been especially helpful, providing assistance and access to the library's fine photography collection. He was also responsible for making a public appeal for additional photographs for this book. Library volunteers Barbara Althouse, Olga Link, and Doris Gable offered valuable assistance with the library's files.

The members of the library board are acknowledged for their support. They are president Judi Flynn, vice president Dennis Schwandt, corresponding secretary Peg Martin, recording secretary Barbara Stevenson, treasurer Roxanne Sockoloskie, and board members Bob Boarts, Gail Hilton, Linda Jones, Mel Keen, and Patti Jo Ziegler.

The Parkesburg Free Library attains its stated mission of providing the borough of Parkesburg and surrounding communities with books, materials, and information necessary for personal growth and lifelong learning. The library's collection contains more than 30,000 volumes. Its staff seeks to guide community and business members to the information they request, including popular culture and current trends.

The majority of the photographs, unless otherwise noted, are from the Parkesburg Free Library collection. Two community members, Gerald L. Treadway and Bill Wilde, made available photographs from their wonderful collections. Treadway is an author and a collector of Parkesburg photographs, documents, and artifacts. He opened his collection and offered valuable information on the background of photographs and borough history. Wilde was also generous with his time and made his family's collection available for this book. They both also aided in the identification of locations and people in the photographs.

David Jones, president of Parkesburg Borough Council, provided background material for the book project. Also, the community of Parkesburg has been supportive of this project and many have offered encouragement and assistance.

—Bruce Edward Mowday, June 2009

INTRODUCTION

When Arcadia Publishing and Parkesburg Free Library director Tom Knecht asked me to join them in the production of this book on the borough of Parkesburg, I readily agreed. Besides being a great community worthy of an Arcadia pictorial history book, Parkesburg has a number of personal connections for me.

Some of my relatives, including my cousin Judy Dougherty and her husband, Denny, live in the borough. My grandfather Raymond C. Mowday Sr. was also from Parkesburg, and he met my grandmother Anna while roller-skating at the Crystal Springs rink just after the conclusion of World War I. They were married on September 2, 1922. The ice-cream store on Route 10 just south of the intersection of Valley Road was a favorite stop of mine as a youngster during the summer months. The ice-cream stand was started by the Hawk family, who also owned a drugstore in Parkesburg.

The vast photographic collection of the Parkesburg Free Library contains many excellent scenes of early life in Parkesburg. During its years of existence, Parkesburg has been a tight-knit community, as depicted in a number of scenes in this book. The residents have been patriotic, as shown by the dedication of the World War I monument and the photographs of a fund-raiser sponsored by the Lions Club that took place during World War II at the Parkesburg Iron Company's old gymnasium.

The early growth of Parkesburg came about by pioneering settlers and later with the establishment of the railroad and a number of businesses, especially the Parkesburg Iron Company. The company and its leaders were visionaries, as one of the first airfields in Chester County was built in a borough field. The iron company also fielded a fine semiprofessional baseball team that played a number of professional teams. Connie Mack brought his Philadelphia professionals to Parkesburg. Talented local squads and even a Cuban national team played the iron company representatives.

Parkesburg is located in the western section of Chester County, one of the most scenic and prosperous sections of the nation. The townships surrounding Parkesburg are rich in agriculture, while the eastern section of the county has many large and successful companies.

Parkesburg bills itself as the economic and cultural center of the Octorara Creek area and invites people to visit and experience its small-town hospitality. It was settled before the Revolutionary War and was first known as Fountain Inn, after a tavern that was constructed in the 1730s and still stands. Many of the early settlements in Chester County were named after taverns. West Chester, the county seat of Chester County, was first named Turk's Head after a tavern.

According to the written history of Parkesburg published on the borough's Web site, the early settlers were predominantly of Scottish-Irish descent, migrating from the area of New Castle, Delaware. New Castle was the destination for some of the families that received land grants from William Penn in the 1600s.

The following part of this introduction is from the Web site www.parkesburg.boroughs.org:

John G. Parke, from whom the Borough got its name, was a noted politician from a prominent family in the area. A relative, General John G. Parke, served during the Civil War and played a prominent role in a number of important campaigns, including Vicksburg, the Wilderness, Spotsylvania and Petersburg.

Throughout the 19th century, the small community rapidly expanded. The prominent Fountain Inn ceased operation as a tavern around 1836 and became Parkesburg's first Post Office. As the population of the town grew, many new industries were attracted there. Among these were the railroad workshops of the newly formed Philadelphia and Columbia Railroad. Some of the oldest photographs in this book are of the railroad shops. The railroad played an important part in Parkesburg's development.

The tracks of the Philadelphia and Columbia were laid to Parkesburg in 1831. A state-funded venture, this railroad was coordinated with an extensive canal system. Since Parkesburg was located at one of the highest points along this railroad, it was decided to situate the repair shops there. Good fortune, however, was not to follow the Philadelphia and Columbia. By 1857, the system had gone bankrupt, with portions of the canal, it was sold to the new Pennsylvania Railroad.

The rapid industrial expansion of the Midwest, and the increasing migration of settlers to such large urban centers as Pittsburgh, Cleveland, and Chicago, enabled the Pennsylvania Railroad to develop rapidly. That expansion had an effect on Parkesburg. In 1861, this rapid expansion prompted the railroad to relocate their shops further west to Harrisburg. Still later, the shops were moved to Altoona where they soon gained the reputation as the world's largest railroad repair shops. Historians claim, however, that it was while these shops were in Parkesburg that standardization—the basis for mass production—first got its start.

It was during the early part of this decade that educational institutions began to spring up in the Parkesburg area. Among the most notable of these was the Parkesburg Academy (later renamed the Parkesburg Institute). Chartered in 1858, a Professor Woodruff was named the first principal of the Academy. Fostering an idea which was years ahead of its time, he favored a system of coeducation for the Academy. This brazen idea, however, was rejected by Mr. Woodruff's peers and the Professor was soon out searching for another job. The Parkesburg Academy remained male oriented for some time to come.

In 1872, Horace Beale moved his Iron Works from Hibernia to Parkesburg where they became known, appropriately, as the Parkesburg Iron Company. This move coincided with the secession of the borough from Sadsbury Township. Act 193 of the Pennsylvania Legislature authorized the formation of Parkesburg Borough, and Samuel R. Parkes was elected its first Burgess. He also organized the town's first bank. Parkesburg became a borough in 1894.

The Great Depression of the 1930s brought hard times to Parkesburg, as it did to much of the rest of the country. With the closing of the Iron Mills, many of the Borough's residents were out of work until they found employment at Lukens Steel in Coatesville.

Today, Parkesburg is a center for industries with local as well as national reputations.

—Bruce Edward Mowday, June 2009

One

THE EARLY DAYS

At the dawn of the 20th century, the construction of the railroad running through the middle of town helped to bring prosperity to Parkesburg. Businesses located and expanded in the borough. In this view, a horse-drawn buggy is seen on First Avenue as it passes the new Parkesburg Hotel. The hotel was under construction at the time of the photograph. (Bill Wilde.)

Parkesburg had one of the first airfields in Chester County. Executives of the Parkesburg Iron Company were responsible for many of the developments in the borough, including the airfield. The above photograph is an aerial view of the field. The white circle has the word "Parkesburg" written through its center. The photograph below shows a crowd gathered behind an airplane as it is getting ready for takeoff. The airfield no longer exists at the Parkesburg site. The nearest one is the G. O. Carlson Airport in Valley Township just to the east of Parkesburg.

Early aviation had its share of mishaps, and crashes were more common than they are today. The photograph at right shows one of the airplanes that failed in its landing attempt on the Parkesburg field. The plane is seen crumpled on the ground. The photograph below shows a plane that successfully completed its trip. Some members of the public were on hand to witness the event. Airplanes were not a common sight at the time, so they drew a lot of attention. A number of airplane enthusiasts lived in Chester County during the early 20th century.

The Parkesburg airfield included a hangar for the few planes that were kept at the borough field. The hangar offered shelter from bad weather and a place to repair airplanes. The hangar, which was constructed in 1919, can be seen in the above photograph. Notice that an automobile of the same era is parked next to the hangar and several people are standing in front. The photograph below shows a crowd gathered around a plane at the airport. Judging from the clothes worn by the people, the scene took place after the hangar was constructed.

One of the functions of the airfield at Parkesburg was to provide a place where airplanes delivering the mail could land. In the above 1920s photograph is an airplane belonging to the Universal Air Service. The pilot and passenger are clearly seen. The airplane was not the usual mode of transportation for Parkesburg residents during the early days of the borough. The man and two boys in the photograph below are using the standard horse and buggy to get around the Parkesburg area. (Above, Gerald L. Treadway; below, Bill Wilde.)

The construction of the railroad through Parkesburg and the location of the repair shop in the borough was a boost to economic vitality during its early days. Above is the original repair shop. The photograph is one of the oldest in the book and is rare. The original bell tower can be seen at the top of the building. The image below is from a postcard and shows a trolley at left and the First Avenue section of Parkesburg. (Above, Bill Wilde; below, Gerald L. Treadway.)

Pub. by H. K. Dorsheimer.   Birds-eye View of Parkesburg, Pa.

The residents of Parkesburg needed retail shops to provide food and other necessities of life. They had choices in shopping destinations, as competing stores were located in town. In the above photograph, one of the storekeepers is ready to fill orders. The shelves are well stocked with goods. The photograph below shows the well-stocked drugstore run at the time by Harry Smith. The thriving and growing Parkesburg community at the dawn of the 20th century supported a number of businesses along the main streets of the borough. (Above, Bill Wilde; below, Gerald L. Treadway.)

Hotel Parkesburg.   PARKESBURG, Pa.

The Hotel Parkesburg is pictured in the above image during the early 1900s. It was one of the most modern hotels in Chester County at the time, with telephones and steam heat. The hotel had 34 rooms with private baths, a dining room, and barroom facilities. The livery stable was located at the rear of the hotel. The photograph below was taken about the same time as the hotel photograph. The scene shows West Street toward Second Avenue. The Episcopal church can be seen in the distance. Several homes can also be seen. (Gerald L. Treadway.)

L TO R. C.C. OWENS, STORE OWNER   J. WILSON WRIGHT HOTEL OWNER   HAMMILL BANKER   CIRCA 1890-1900

Three of Parkesburg's business owners are shown in the photograph above. From left to right, they are store owner C. C. Owens, hotel owner J. Wilson Wright, and banker Mr. Hammill. The scene was shot in the late 1800s at the rear of the bank building. The image below is a photograph postcard taken after the new train station opened in 1906. The postcard indicates the station is part of the Pennsylvania Railroad. The Pennsylvania Railroad took over the rails after the company was formed, but it was not the original builder of the line. (Gerald L. Treadway.)

The Parkesburg business district was busy during the day in the early 20th century. One of the most important buildings for business owners and residents was the bank on Main Street. The photograph at left shows the bank building adorned with flags for a special day. It is to the left of the store. The photograph below shows the business scene on the 400 block of First Avenue. At the corner is the Harry Smith drugstore. The interior of the store is shown on page 15. One of the main advertising signs on the outside of the drugstore was for soda water.

The hardware store in Parkesburg contained just about anything needed for a business or home. The interior of the Cromleigh Hardware Store is seen above. All the available space in the store seems to be filled with items, and lanterns and buckets are hung from the ceiling. At the far left is owner Harry Cromleigh. The other two men are unidentified. Many towns at the time had opera houses. Parkesburg's opera house was on First Avenue. The outside of the building was used for advertising. The image below was taken about 1915. The building is now a dental office. (Above, Bill Wilde; below, Gerald L. Treadway.)

The caption on the above photograph indicates the Parkesburg scene could be used for a "movie set." The photograph shows Gay Street in the late 1800s. The Parkesburg bank building can be seen in the upper right. Some of the photographs in this book, including the two on this page, are from the collection of Gerald L. Treadway. His home on Strasburg Avenue is seen in the photograph below. The home was decorated for a World War I celebration. Treadway obtained the photograph from the Matilda Garnett collection. (Below, Gerald L. Treadway.)

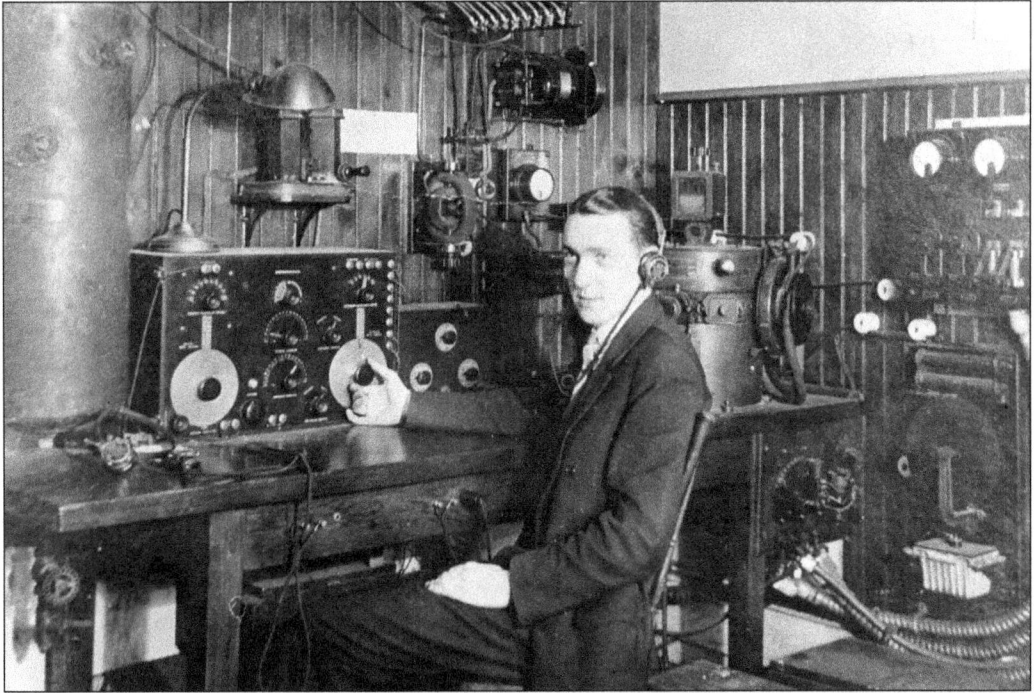

Parkesburg not only had its own airfield in the 1920s but also an experimental radio station. The station had all the modern equipment of the time. The photograph above shows Boyd Cowan and the studio of W3LO-WQAA. He is seated at the control desk with his headphones on and appears to be operating the dials. The photograph below shows the interior of the studio with the radio equipment. The station operated in the time period that Pittsburgh station KDKA made its historic first broadcast of music. The popularity of the medium led to a boom in the manufacturing of radio receivers.

The above photograph shows experimental radio station operator Boyd Cowan broadcasting from the studio of W3LO-WQAA. The radio craze in America took off during the 1920s. The photograph of Cowan was taken at this time. Between 1923 and 1930, more than 60 percent of the families in America purchased radios. Another early Parkesburg scene is captured in the photograph below, which was taken in the late 1800s. The photograph is of a class at the Parkesburg Academy. The academy operated from 1858 until 1885 and was at one time known as the Parkesburg Institute. The school was coeducational, a rarity for the times.

Two

COMMUNITY LIFE

The residents of Parkesburg have a
tradition of taking an active interest in
the well-being of their community. The
borough has held a number of parades
over the years and put on patriotic events.
Shown here is Ira Goldman, owner of the
Parkesburg dress factory, in the 1940s.
He is singing during a Lions Club charity
fund-raising event. (Bill Wilde.)

The photograph above shows workers setting up for the band for a fund-raising event for the Lions Club. A number of charity fund-raising events were held over the years in Parkesburg. This event took place during World War II. The American flag is prominent behind the band chairs, and the Lions Club banner is hung on the lower level. The photograph below is of a "Victory" banner being displayed, while a woman in uniform stands at attention before it. Members of the large crowd can be seen to the right. (Bill Wilde.)

The Lions Club victory charity fund-raising event took place in April 1943 during the middle of World War II. The event drew a large crowd of Parkesburg residents and was held at the basketball gymnasium of the Parkesburg Iron Company. Those attending the event were entertained by a number of acts and speeches. The above photograph shows part of a troupe of dancers that performed for the crowd. The photograph below shows men in uniform holding flags and rifles standing at attention while another solider is speaking to the gathered throng. (Bill Wilde.)

A crowd gathers before a Parkesburg Fire Company truck in the above photograph, which appears to have been taken during World War II at a community event. Notice one of the young men above is wearing a navy cap. The fire department played a major role in the social life of Parkesburg residents, especially early in the 20th century. The image below shows a group of Civil War reenactors.

All across America during World War II, patriotic citizens were saving valuable material for the war effort. The above photograph shows J. Ross Owens standing with his hands on his hips in front of a pile of donated household utensils from Parkesburg residents. The material was given for the military effort. Youngsters on the road are looking down on Owens. The photograph below shows the Parkesburg bank building on Main Street in 1919. It is decorated as part of a celebration for the conclusion of World War I. (Gerald L. Treadway.)

Young racers took to the streets of Parkesburg in September 1947 for a soapbox derby competition. The above photograph shows the racers and their cars ready to begin the competition at the starting line and an audience of community members gathered around the racers, waiting for the starting flag. The winner of the race was Donald Daller, second from left. He called his winning car "Brown Beauty." In the photograph below, a band plays in the street in front of the Parkesburg Iron Company. (Above, Bill Wilde.)

Bands played big parts in many celebrations in Parkesburg over the years and continue to do so today. Community and company bands formed in the borough and surrounding towns, and high school bands practiced and played in parades and other events. The Parkesburg High School band is shown above in 1935 at the veterans' administration hospital in Coatesville. The band shown below played in the first half of the 20th century in Parkesburg at a gymnasium. (Above, Gerald L. Treadway.)

Above, Parkesburg students gather outside the school while waiting for classes to begin. One person identified standing to the right near the building's wall is Joan Pringle. The photograph below shows a Parkesburg school band from a different era in the school gymnasium, which is decorated for an event. A majorette is seen at right, and cheerleaders sporting a *P* on their uniforms are seen in the background.

Parkesburg residents have long taken pride in their children's education. The tradition of educational excellence began with the forming of the Parkesburg Academy, and it continues today. The photographs on this page are of Parkesburg school classes. Above, the students appear to be standing at attention. The teacher is on the left. Some of the boys in the first row of the photograph below favor the folded-arms pose. Also one girl in the last row has a large bow in her hair.

The photographic archives of the Parkesburg Free Library contain a number of class photographs of Parkesburg schools. The above photograph shows smiling students. The teacher, shown to the right in the back row, is more somber. The photograph below shows students in the front row enjoying posing for the camera. The teacher, with her hands on her hips, is seen standing at right in the back row. Bows were in style, as two young girls can be seen with them in their hair.

Reunion photographs are as important as class photographs to many former students. The nine men shown in the above photograph were members of the 1922 graduating class in Parkesburg. As seen in photographs on previous pages, the students have aged a little over the years. A second photograph of the 1922 graduates is shown below. The photographs on this page were taken during the class reunion held in 1970.

Sporting events have played a big part in the Parkesburg community. The Parkesburg Iron Works Company fielded a baseball team that was competitive against some of the professional teams of the time. The above photograph shows a group of youngsters affiliated with the Lions Club baseball team gathering at a borough park. Two of these people played a lot of baseball during their lives: Wayne Thomas (third row, right) and Sonny Skiles (second row, second from left). Below is a Parkesburg tennis team, photographed around 1910. (Above, Bill Wilde; below, Gerald L. Treadway.)

Community life during the early part of the 20th century included events held at the Parkesburg Iron Company. The next three photographs are of a lawn party held in 1924 at the office building in the rear of the company's complex. Refreshments were part of the day. The event could have also been a fund-raiser, as a "Toy Shop" sign is seen to the right above, along with three women to the left with serving trays. The photograph below shows four women who appear to be selling baked goods. (Gerald L. Treadway.)

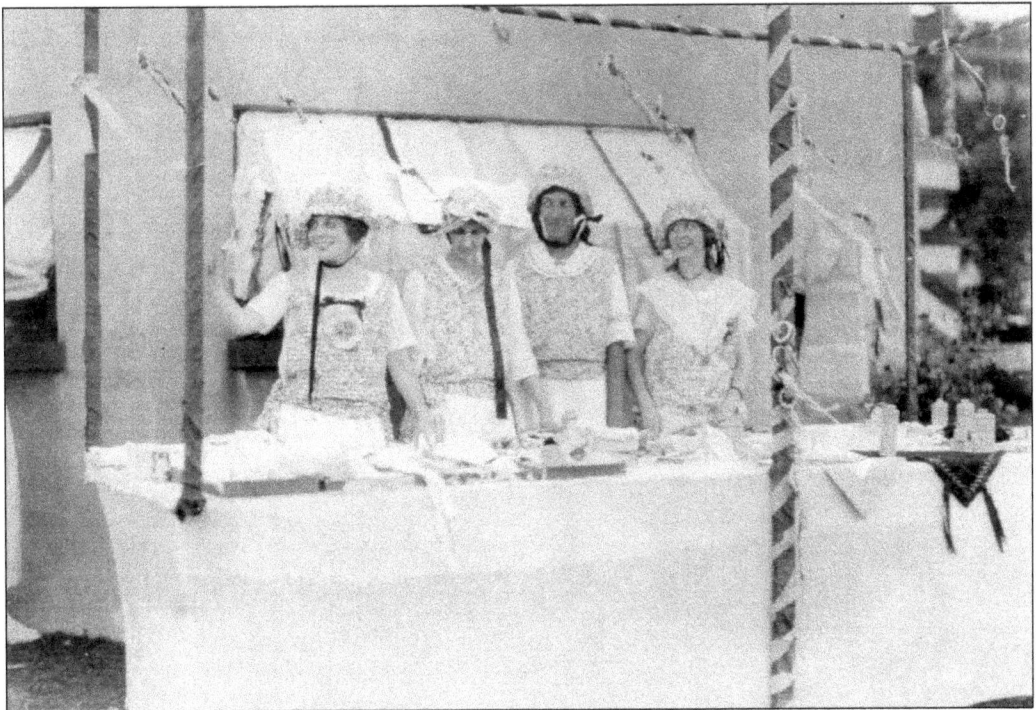

Women enjoy the 1924 lawn party at the Parkesburg Iron Company in the above photograph. A table full of flowers is positioned between the two groups of women. Gerald L. Treadway stated that these lawn party photographs and several others in this book were originally obtained from Art and Bitsy Schravesande. Seen below, circus acts were captured on film during a 1953 visit to Parkesburg, as they were about to entertain the borough residents. (Above, Gerald L. Treadway.)

Holidays, especially the Christmas season, are special times in Parkesburg. Parades and other celebrations are held. At least one winter in the 1950s fulfilled the wish of those dreaming of a white Christmas. The above photograph shows snow and Christmas lights hung above First Avenue. Parkesburg is located in a section of the country where the Christmas season can be cold and snowy or warm and dry. The photograph at right shows Santa Claus visiting one Christmas holiday event and making a young Parkesburg resident happy. The Lions Club banner can be seen in the background. (Above, Gerald L. Treadway.)

Private organizations and service clubs played a large part in community life in Parkesburg. In the photograph above, three women receive recognition during an event at the American Legion. The woman at left is presenting gifts. The photograph below shows some of those gathered for a dinner at the American Legion. The American Legion was chartered by Congress in 1919 as a patriotic, wartime veterans' organization devoted to mutual helpfulness. It is a nonprofit community-service organization that now numbers nearly three million members, including men and women, in nearly 15,000 American Legion posts worldwide.

Community events in Parkesburg drew dignitaries from across the region. The photograph at right shows Gen. Smedley Darlington Butler of West Chester. He was known as the "Fighting Quaker" and was the most decorated Marine in history at the time of his death. He also served as director of public safety in Philadelphia. Butler attended the June 1935 dedication of the Parkesburg Fire Company. Also shown with Butler are Alfred M. Clarrey and Jerry DaPrato. The photograph below shows four women enjoying a dinner at the American Legion post in Parkesburg.

Bands of many different types performed in Parkesburg over the years. Above is one of the most unusual ones, identified on the banner as the Heberling Zobo Band. Besides the banner, the band also carries an oversized watch. "Zobo" bands appear to be offbeat types of organizations. One was formed in New York State in the latter part of the 20th century that performed jazz and blues. Below is the more traditional Mendelsshon Concert Band in May 1902.

Three

COMMUNITY LEADERS

Many community leaders helped to make Parkesburg successful. John G. Parke, from whom the borough received its name, was a noted politician from a prominent family in the area. His relative Gen. John Grubb Parke (pictured here) served during the Civil War and played a major role in such campaigns as Fredericksburg, Vicksburg, the Wilderness, Spotsylvania, and Petersburg.

The members of the borough council make the day-to-day decisions on the running of Parkesburg. The positions are elected, and the members have the duty to make decisions that affect the everyday lives of residents. They have the ability to raise money to provide for essential services, including police protection. Pictured above are the members of the 1945 council. The photograph below contains members of the 1964 council and two of Parkesburg's past mayors, Paul Stoner (center) and Bill Stroup (right).

The Parkesburg Fire Company has been a community leader for more than a century. A charter was granted to the Parkesburg Hose Company No. 1 by the Chester County Court on June 11, 1894. The above photograph shows some of the company's officials in the 1950s. Those identified include Delano Large, Jim Wilde (back row, left), Marris Mullen (back row, far right), and Harry Cromleigh (first row, far right). The photograph below was taken at a borough council function.

In 1872, Horace A. Beale moved his ironworks from nearby Hibernia to Parkesburg, where it became known as the Parkesburg Iron Company. The above photograph shows Horace A. Beale Jr. driving. Beale Jr. was president of the iron company and also a director of the National Bank of Chester Valley and Parkesburg Electric Lighting, Heating and Power Company. Joining him in the front of the car is Winfield Coleman, and in back are J. Evans Wright (left) and Alexander Sellers. The car won a race between Camden and Atlantic City in New Jersey. Below is an image from a postcard of the Beale home in Parkesburg. (Gerald L. Treadway.)

Four

LANDMARKS

The railroad helped bring prosperity to the borough of Parkesburg. The tracks of the Philadelphia and Columbia Railroad were laid to Parkesburg in 1831. Later the rail line became part of the Pennsylvania Railroad. The old Pennsylvania Railroad station is seen in this photograph, which was taken prior to 1906. (Gerald L. Treadway.)

As a settled community, Parkesburg predates the Revolutionary War. Parkesburg is located in Chester County, one of the original three counties founded by William Penn. The borough was first known as Fountain Inn, named after an inn that was constructed about 1734 and stands today as a private residence at 131–133 Main Street. The above photograph shows a view of the structure as a private residence. The view below shows the interior of the old inn, including a fireplace.

Above is a side view of the Fountain Inn. The stone walls are distinctive parts of the old home, dating from the early 18th century. The first settlers of the area were predominantly of Scottish-Irish descent, who migrated north on the Gap-Newport Pike, now Route 41, from New Castle, Delaware. Below is a full view of the fireplace from the old inn. The room is also decorated with antiques, including lamps and pictures.

PRESBYTERIAN CHURCH, PARKESBURG, Pa.

Churches constitute many of the landmarks in Parkesburg. The distinctive buildings of the churches are located throughout the borough streets. At left is the Presbyterian church on Strasburg Avenue. The building fronts on Main Street and was constructed in the 1800s. Presbyterianism evolved primarily in Scotland, and many of the first settlers of Parkesburg came from Scotland. The photograph below shows the Methodist church, which is located on Main Street. (Gerald L. Treadway.)

The photographs on this page were taken during the groundbreaking for the Parkesburg Baptist Church. The photograph at right is of a young woman, believed to be the daughter of the church's pastor. She begins the building process by shoveling a load of dirt. Below, a crowd gathers for the event. The members of the group all seem to be dressed in their Sunday best. The Baptist Church was founded by John Smyth in Holland in 1609, as a separatist from the Church of England, and by Roger Williams in Rhode Island in 1638. (Bill Wilde.)

A mystery involves the home at 345 Main Street in the heart of Parkesburg. Murals were found on its interior walls in July 1963. The person who painted the murals is unknown, as is the exact time the murals were painted, but they were preserved as much as possible. The Commonwealth of Pennsylvania became interested in the murals, and they are now housed in a Harrisburg museum. The home where the murals were found is pictured above. One of the murals is pictured at left.

Here are two more of the murals. The above photograph shows a hole in the mural and the wall to allow for a heating pipe to exit the room. The scene suggests a Caribbean island. Palm trees can be seen along the shore. There is a small island in the harbor and the distant shore has an outline of a large coast. The mural at right shows a harbor town with ships. A different type of tree is shown in this mural, and it could be an early American seaport town.

The murals on the walls of the home at 345 Main Street are believed to have been painted by an itinerant artist in the 19th century. But the identity of the artist is not known. The murals were removed from the home and are now housed in the William Penn Museum in Harrisburg. The photograph at left shows a mural wrapped around a wall covering, featuring a volcano scene. The mural below suggests a European scene by the construction of the houses and the mountains in the background.

Parkesburg Public School, Parkesburg, Pa.

Pub. by H. K. Dorsheimer

Schools are landmarks in most communities, as they are in Parkesburg. Above is a postcard of the Parkesburg Public School that borders Strasburg Avenue. Below is a view of the school from the west side along Strasburg Avenue. The site was abandoned but turned into housing for seniors, with 34 apartments being built. The project included the adaptive reuse of the elementary school. The new construction includes a community room, utilizing the school's existing high ceilings, plaster moldings, and stage. The housing complex also has an outreach clinic of Brandywine Hospital on the premises.

Educational institutions began to open in Parkesburg in the mid-19th century. Among the most notable was the Parkesburg Academy, later renamed the Parkesburg Institute. The school was chartered in 1858, and the first principal was Prof. W. W. Woodruff, who favored a system of coeducation at the academy. His idea was rejected, and he soon left the academy, which only admitted boys for a number of years. This photograph of the school was taken after it was no longer in use.

The Morris-Hall property on South Gay Street was a landmark in Parkesburg. The above photograph shows the home, which no longer exists. Pictured below are the Morris-Hall gardens on the grounds. The property was used as a small, exclusive resort at one time, and the gardens were one of its main attractions. The bedrooms were billed as large and well ventilated. The hospitality of the dining room was extended to small groups for banquets or informal gatherings.

The Beale mansion on Route 10 or 200 South Church Street was known for a time as the Fireside Restaurant and then the Chateau Restaurant. Recently Bill Wilde and his son took over the mansion and opened Beale Manor for catering and special events. In 1896, Horace A. Beale, iron master of the Parkesburg Iron Company, completed the reconstruction of the former Parke mansion. The ornate Victorian-style rooms can still be seen at Beale Manor. The above photograph shows the Fireside Restaurant as it looked in September 1966. The photograph below is from the same era.

The Parkesburg Iron Company had multiple mills, forges, and charcoal houses during the early 20th century. The image below shows the dam that helped the company secure water for its operations. Pictured above is a scene of the gardens at the Beale home. The Beale grounds were well kept and had one of the finest gardens in Parkesburg at the time. The residence has been operated as different restaurants over the years and now is home to a catering and special events business. (Below, Gerald L. Treadway.)

PARKESBURG DAM,
PARKESBURG, Pa.

Dominating the landscape of Parkesburg in the 20th century was the Parkesburg Iron Company. The business was a major employer and also utilized a considerable amount of land in the borough. The above photograph shows a part of the company around the dawn of the 20th century. The Parkesburg firehouse now sits on the site. Below is a scene of Parkesburg looking north from the railroad tracks. Bill Wilde's family's funeral home is to the right of Culvert Street, which intersects with Main Street. (Gerald L. Treadway.)

Looking North from Penna. R. R. Station.   PARKESBURG, Pa.

Parkesburg's prosperity was evident in the early 20th century. The town had an opera house and movie theater. Pictured at right is Edith Moore, the motion picture machine operator for the Lyric Moving Picture Parlor in 1919. She was the only licensed female motion picture machine operator in Pennsylvania. The Lyric Moving Picture Parlor was located on Main Street and is shown below. The photographs originally belonged to Martha Ross, who is related to Moore. (Gerald L. Treadway.)

Grand-:-Opening
OF THE
"**LYRIC**"
Moving Picture Parlor
Main Street, Parkesburg, Pa.

Saturday, Oct. 11th, '13

Concert by Prof. Harris and His Band
During the Entire Evening
Matinee Saturdays at 2.30. Monday, Thursday and Sat-
urday Evenings at 7 o'clock.

Best and Newest Reels
at Each and Every Show.

Five Reels to Amuse and Instruct
Assisted by a Victor Victrola

WATCH OUR BULLETINS
Every Day. Something New Every Time! A Scream
for Everybody! Don't miss seeing our shows
MONDAYS, THURSDAYS and SATURDAYS.

Good Music! Lots to Laugh at!
Be Sure and Meet Me at the

"LYRIC".

Saturday Afternoon October 11
at 2.30 O'clock, and we will arrange to be on
hand SATURDAY EVENING at 7 o'clock.

5 Big Reels and 3 Big Shows

ADMISSION:
Saturday Matinees,   Adults, 10c.; Children, 5c.
Monday and Thursday Eve'gs., Adults, 10c.; Children 5c.
Saturday Evenings, Everybody 10c.

The opening of the Lyric Moving Picture Parlor and the end of the movie theater are shown here. At left is the grand opening flyer for the Parkesburg theater. The opening day was Saturday, October 11, 1913, and the show consisted of a concert by Professor Harris and his band and the "best and newest reels to amuse and entertain." The cost to see the show was 10¢ for adults and 5¢ for children. The photograph below was taken in 1958 after the roof of the theater collapsed. The building was located at West First Avenue and West Street. The photographs were originally part of the Martha Ross collection. (Gerald L. Treadway.)

A main gathering point in Parkesburg for many years was the fountain installed at Strasburg Avenue and Main Street as a watering place for horses. It is shown around 1919. The need for the fountain went away as the town became a hub of modern transportation, with a trolley line and railroad stop. Below is a store on Front Street that was later turned into a residence. Two people are standing in front of the building. (Right, Gerald L. Treadway; below, Bill Wilde.)

Shown above is Wright's Hotel decked out for a celebration. Above, the cars shown to the left indicate the event took place in the early 20th century, possibly in connection with a World War I celebration. A group of residents is crowded on the second-floor balcony with many more people below them. They appear to be dressed in their finest clothes. The hotel no longer exists. Below is the Presbyterian church on Strasburg Avenue during a World War I celebration. The building later became a Masonic hall. (Above, Bill Wilde; below, Gerald L. Treadway.)

The Parkesburg Baptist Church was constructed in the early part of the 20th century. The above photograph shows the building shortly after construction was completed. The borough's Mennonite Church at East Second Avenue and Route 10 is shown below. The church was constructed in the 1950s and recently rebuilt. The Mennonites arrived in America with the help of William Penn. The church reports more than 100,000 members in the United States and about 1.3 million members worldwide. (Gerald L. Treadway.)

Mennonite Church, Parkesburg, Pa.

The firehouse's construction in the 1930s was part of the federal Works Progress Administration program. The above photograph shows the building, which at one time functioned as Parkesburg's borough hall. The Works Progress Administration was the largest New Deal agency created by Pres. Franklin D. Roosevelt's administration and funded by Congress as part of the 1935 Emergency Relief Appropriation Act. The program employed millions of people. Pictured below is Parvin Place on West Main Street, which was owned by the Smith family, original landowners in Parkesburg. (Gerald L. Treadway.)

Episcopal Church, Parkesburg, Pa.

Parkesburg's Episcopal church, pictured above, was built before the dawn of the 20th century and is located at Second Avenue and West Street. The church contains the Beale memorial tower. The Beale family brought the iron company to Parkesburg and manufactured locomotive boiler tubes for many years. Horace A. Beale was known for his many acts of charity and kindliness toward the poor. The borough's Catholic church and rectory are shown below. (Gerald L. Treadway.)

CATHOLIC CHURCH AND RECTORY, PARKESBURG, PENNA.

These photographs show the Johnstone engineering site. The rarely seen photograph above shows the Johnstone site as it was in 1906 when the Parkesburg Iron Company owned the property. First Avenue is located in the foreground and Gay Street is to the right. Johnstone became the owners of the property in 1946 after the demise of the iron company. Below is the Johnstone engineering building, which has since become Parkesburg Borough Hall. (Gerald L. Treadway.)

Parkesburg's northern side sits upon a hill. Above is a scene from about 1910 looking south from the Parkesburg school steps. The town has grown since the photograph was taken, and now it has a population of more than 3,000 people, according to the latest census. It is 1.2 square miles in size. Below is the American Legion hall, which sits in the eastern section of the borough. The building has been used for many celebrations and events over the years. (Above, Gerald L. Treadway.)

The sketch above is of the old state railroad repair shops located in Parkesburg in the 1800s. In 1835, the land came from the family of John G. Parke, for whom Parkesburg was named. The repair shops operated until 1859 when they were moved to Harrisburg. The site was then used by N. P. Boyer for a publishing plant. Later the Parkesburg Iron Company took over the land and operated there from 1872 until 1926, when the Johnstone Company operated at the site. Below is the Parkesburg garage. In a window is a decal that indicates the shop is affiliated with Ford. The photographs were originally from the Larry Welsch collection. (Gerald L. Treadway.)

Five

BASEBALL

Horace A. Beale Jr. was the person responsible for bringing many innovations to Parkesburg during the early part of the 20th century. He was president of the Parkesburg Iron Company and son of the company's founder. He liked to race cars, and he built the borough's airport. He also formed a semiprofessional baseball team that represented the iron company. Pictured here is baseball player Sid Agnew of the iron company team.

The semiprofessional baseball team representing the Parkesburg Iron Company played many professional teams and all-star clubs from the region. International teams also played in Parkesburg. Above are members of one of the Parkesburg teams. The uniforms denote that they played during the early part of the 20th century. The image below shows the baseball field where the iron company team challenged many of those professional players. The field was located close to where the Parkesburg Free Library stands today.

Many famous professional teams traveled to Parkesburg to play the iron company team. One of the most famous individuals was Cornelius McGillicuddy Sr., better known as "Connie Mack." He played professional baseball for 11 seasons but gained his reputation as a manager and owner. He managed the Philadelphia Athletics for the club's first 50 seasons and retired at age 87 following the 1950 season. He was the first manager to win the World Series three times and was elected to the Baseball Hall of Fame in 1937. McGillicuddy is pictured above in Parkesburg in 1919. At right is iron company player Fred Moore.

Parkesburg Iron Company Baseball Field where such teams as the New York Ship, New York Giants and the World's Champions (1919), Cincinnati Reds, were entertained.

The above photograph shows a view of the Parkesburg Iron Company field from beyond the outfield walls. A game was being played at the time it was taken. The information on the photograph indicates that many well-known teams played on this field, including the New York Ship, the New York Giants, and the 1919 World Series champion Cincinnati Reds. A team of Cuban all-stars also was reported to have played the iron company team, which had a reputation of being a great semiprofessional team. Pictured at left is outfielder George Silknetter.

Every baseball team needs a batboy, and the team representing the Parkesburg Iron Company had Charles Coleman for a number of years. The young Coleman is shown at right. As a batboy, he was in charge of helping the players during the game. One of the players was Ted Baldwin, shown below.

The long and proud tradition of playing baseball in Parkesburg continues to this day in the borough. The above photograph shows a baseball trophy being presented during a recent ceremony in Parkesburg. Baseball has thrived in Parkesburg since the time professional players journeyed to the borough for games in the early part of the 20th century.

Six

PARKESBURG IRON COMPANY

The Horace A. Beale family brought the Parkesburg Iron Company to the borough during the 1800s, and it was the main business here for decades. The company manufactured locomotive boiler tubes for many years that most of the rail lines in the United States used at the time. Here one of the workers is seen with some scrap metal.

The above photograph shows the Parkesburg Iron Company and notes that it operated from 1872 to 1926 in the borough. Visible is the railroad line that ran through the company. The railroad played an important part in the growth of the iron company and also of the borough of Parkesburg. The company was a large employer of residents from the borough and the surrounding area. The photograph below shows one of the employees working before a hot furnace. The construction of the locomotive boiler tubes required hot and demanding work.

The work at the Parkesburg Iron Company was backbreaking at times and required the handling of white-hot material, as evidenced by the employees above. They are operating in tandem on one of the company's machines. The photograph below shows workers with shovels outside one of the company's buildings. Three of the men are identified as Bill Black, Harry Gillespie, and Abe Wood.

The Parkesburg Iron Company (pictured above) occupied a large amount of the land in the borough of Parkesburg. President Horace A. Beale Jr. had a number of interests, including cars, planes, and radio. One of his other interests was baseball, and the field can be seen to the right. The manufacturing of the products at the plant required a lot of material. The photograph below shows the many tubes that were kept in one of the company's buildings.

The Parkesburg Iron Company had a reputation for producing quality products. Many of the train lines across the country used the locomotive boiler tubes produced in the borough plant. Parkesburg has been connected with railroads since the beginning of the 19th century. Above, one of the company officials inspects the locomotive tubes. The official is conferring with three of the floor plant workers. Below, floor workers attend to one of the machines. The work at the Parkesburg Iron Company was labor intensive.

The Parkesburg Iron Company did not rely on the local police force for enforcement on the grounds of the company. President Horace A. Beale Jr. had the company form its own group of officers, who are pictured above about the time of World War I. They had horses and motorcycles to ride. The aerial shot below as taken about the same time. The company's water tower and its shadow can be seen to the bottom right. (Above, Gerald L. Treadway.)

The Parkesburg Iron Company operation expanded during the years it operated in the borough. The company began in 1872 under the direction of founder Horace A. Beale. He was born in Philadelphia and had his first job with the Phoenix Iron Company and then worked in nearby Coatesville. He also owned a company in Maryland and was involved in companies in the Chester County communities of Thorndale and Hibernia before establishing the Parkesburg company. The above photograph shows the construction of a plant building around 1908. The photograph below shows the community north of the iron company. (Above, Gerald L. Treadway.)

The manufacturing of the tubes for the railroad engines required exacting and precise work. A lot of man-hours were needed, and company supervisors kept a constant watch on the progress of the work. Above, one supervisor is on the floor of the plant being given a report. The photograph below shows completed tubes loaded on railcars and ready for shipment throughout the country. To the right is the watchtower used by the company's police force.

The employees of the Parkesburg Iron Company worked hard for their wages. The above photograph shows two workers unloading large baskets of charcoal. They are transporting it on a wagon from a storage area to the main plant. The material was needed to make the company's products. At right, four men take part in the surface inspection of skelp. Skelp, or scelp, is a band of iron commonly forged from melted scrap iron. Pipe and tubing were made with this material.

The Parkesburg Iron Company hall was used for many events in the borough. Basketball games and celebrations of all kinds took place in the company building, which was destroyed by fire in 1957. Pictured above is the building as it was being consumed by flames. The hall was not rebuilt. The photograph at left shows a controlled fire at the No. 145 forge of the iron company. The forge was an essential part of the manufacturing process for the company. One of the workers in the photograph is identified as Aaron McGuigan. (Above, Gerald L. Treadway.)

Seven

CRYSTAL SPRINGS

The residents of Parkesburg and the surrounding areas gathered at Crystal Springs Park on the northern boundary of the borough. Pictured here is a large crowd on a nice summer's day. Children, young adults, and older adults can be seen enjoying the activities.

Many activities were offered at Crystal Springs Park, just off Route 10 in Parkesburg, during the early part of the 20th century. Above, three men pose for the camera in front of the boardwalk. The information on the photograph says a game of ball toss is seen behind the men, to the left is the Skee-Ball area, and to the right is the shooting gallery. Below, four men are seen boating on the park's lake around 1915. (Below, Gerald L. Treadway.)

An early view of Crystal Springs Park is seen in the above photograph, taken about 1915. Three men are standing near where water from the springs can be drawn. The photograph below of the midway portion of the park was taken about 15 years later. The signs in the photograph note that sandwiches and coffee could be purchased at two of the stands. The park no longer exists, and today the Heritage Crystal Springs apartments stand on the site. (Gerald L. Treadway.)

The spring at Crystal Springs Park is captured above in the 1920s. Behind the woman in the photograph is a machine to dispense water. Two men stand in front of the park buildings in the photograph below. The park was used for different events, including Chester County's Old Fiddlers' Picnic. One poster for the August 7, 1937, event said children were admitted free but adults had to pay 10¢. Musical talent, dancing, radio players, and fun for everyone were promised for the picnic. William T. G. Young was named as the manager, and Mrs. Charles Davis was the secretary. (Above, Gerald L. Treadway.)

Crystal Springs Park, on the northern border of the borough of Parkesburg, was a popular meeting place for friends and courting couples. Sitting on the park bridge above are four men and two boys. From left to right are (sitting) unidentified and Russell Souillard; (standing) Bill Souillard, Lee Conover, Wilber White, and Harry McMullen. The photograph below shows Conover and Bill White. The others are unidentified.

Crystal Springs Park offered many different activities, including a roller-skating rink. The roller-skating rink was the place where the grandparents of the author first met. Here three men pose at a swing set. From front to back are Bill Souillard, Harry McMullen, and Lee Conover.

Eight

FIRE DEPARTMENT

The community of Parkesburg is proud of its fire department, which has offered many years of service. The community has generously supported it. The members of the fire company also like to show off its equipment during community parades. Pictured here is a ladder truck with four members ready for a parade in 1959. The truck has American flags on the front bumper.

The Parkesburg Fire Company has been participating in community parades for almost a century throughout the region. Members have ventured far from the borough's boundaries to march in neighboring parades. Above, the company's motorized equipment and firefighting unit get ready for an event in 1918. The company has been able to serve the community because of dedicated volunteers who handle many tasks in the firehouse. The photograph below shows Gertrude Miller receiving an award from Robert Gillespie Jr. in 1972.

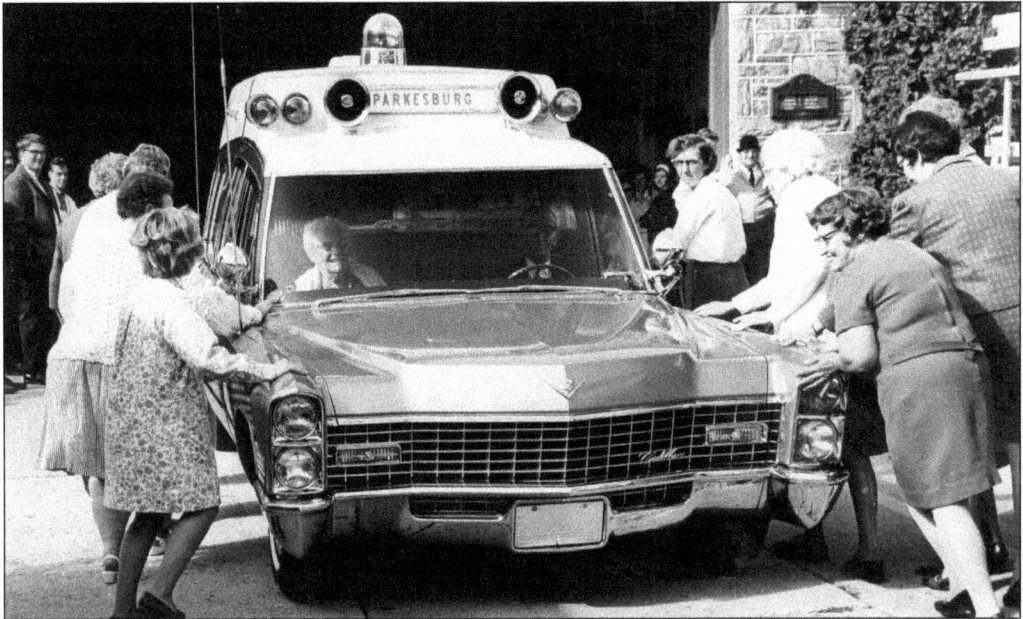

The Parkesburg Fire Company has hosted many different kinds of celebrations, including dinners and other events for members and supporters. Some of the events involve the whole community, and others are for the personal milestones of those associated with the fire company. The above photograph shows a happy couple being given a push by friends in a fire company vehicle. The photograph below shows fire company official Ed Patterson (with the microphone) addressing the crowd at a department dinner.

A major community event took place in Parkesburg in 1934 when the borough started to build a new fire facility to house the company's vehicles. The expanded fire department was needed as the borough's population increased. Above, a large crowd turned out to see the first shovelful of dirt being turned for the building at the groundbreaking ceremony. The photograph below shows the completed building some years after the construction, with three of the department's vehicles.

The Parkesburg Fire Company volunteers are all ages. There was even a junior firemen's program in the borough. The volunteers put in many long hours, making sure the department's vehicles are in running condition to fight borough fires when needed. The fire company's duty is to protect the more than 3,000 residents of the borough of Parkesburg. The above photograph shows four firemen receiving trophies for their hard work. The identifications of those pictured are unknown. In the photograph below, smiling fire company officials get ready for a banquet.

The May 18, 1967, Parkesburg Fire Company awards banquet brought smiles to award winners and members of their families. The photograph at left shows fire company officials and the award winners with certificates and trophies. The man seated is former borough chief of police Earl Shipman. The fire company has had a number of vehicles over the years. The photograph below shows the fire company's second pumper, which served the Parkesburg community for 16 years from 1924 until 1940. The company raises money to replace vehicles that are outdated or in need of replacement. Today's vehicles can cost hundreds of thousands of dollars.

Fire companies in Parkesburg and throughout the area have expanded their bands of firefighting volunteers over the years. At one point, only men were members of the department and fought fires. For years, women's auxiliaries were formed and provided valuable support for the operation of the fire departments. The above photograph shows five members of the Parkesburg Fire Company's Junior Fire Ladies organization in June 1970. In April of the same year, a banquet was held, and the winners of the junior firefighters of the year award were given trophies, pictured below.

Volunteer fire companies were first formed in the United States by Benjamin Franklin in Philadelphia in the 1700s to protect life and property. The main duty of the companies is to fight fires. Above, Parkesburg firefighters respond to a blaze in January 1973 at a home on Upper Valley Road. Smoke is coming from the roof area, and firefighters are putting a ladder against one of the walls. The photograph below shows the aftermath of a September 1967 fire that caused $60,000 in damages to the building.

Nine

COMMUNITY SCENES

The borough of Parkesburg was named after noted local politician John G. Parke. This photograph shows the original Parke home on East Main Street and was taken prior to 1900. (Gerald L. Treadway.)

Parkesburg has always been a family-friendly community. The photograph at left shows Charles Ross Owens holding his pet while standing in front of a store on Main Street. The photograph below shows the bank building with a hitching post in front of the two men. The store's windows are full of posters and other items. Parkesburg had a thriving business community at the dawn of the 20th century, the period when the Parkesburg Iron Company was employing residents and providing an income for many in the town. (Below, Gerald L. Treadway.)

Trolley tracks can be seen in the middle of First Avenue in the above photograph, taken during the early 1900s looking west. The borough was authorized by the Pennsylvania legislature in 1872. Prior to its formation, the town was part of Sadsbury Township. The borough council is the ruling body for the town. The photograph below shows its members on January 4, 1954, probably during the swearing-in and reorganizational meeting for the council. (Above, Gerald L. Treadway.)

Parkesburg was first known as Fountain Inn, after a tavern constructed about 1734. The inn operated as a tavern until 1836, and then it is said to have been the borough's first post office. The above photograph shows another famous Parkesburg restaurant, the Fireside Inn, which has been run as different restaurants over the years and now is a catering and special events venue. The photograph below shows the Parkesburg Presbyterian Church. Parkesburg is home to a number of different religions, and churches are seen in almost all segments of the borough.

STRASBURG AVE.

SCHOOL HOUSE

FIRST AVE. LOOKING WEST

CHURCH OF THE ASCENSION, 2ND AVE.

LOOKING NORTH-EAST FROM STATION

GAY ST. LOOKING NORTH

LOOKING N.E. FROM 2ND AVE.

PARKESBURG IRON CO. MILLS.

RECTORY AND CHURCH OF OUR LADY OF CONSOLATION

Views of

LOOKING DOWN STRASBURG AVE

PARKESBURG, PA.

The postcard image on this page shows 10 views of Parkesburg. Two of the borough's churches are depicted. Also shown is the Parkesburg Iron Company, the main business in the town during the late 19th century. A school and street scenes are shown on the postcard. (Bruce Edward Mowday.)

Horace A. Beale Jr., president of the Parkesburg Iron Company, was known as a sportsman. His interests included aviation, and he was responsible for establishing of one of the first airfields in Chester County. It is pictured above in the early 1920s with a plane preparing for a flight. Notice the shadows of two men in the front center of the photograph. The circus was also an attraction for residents. The photograph at left shows a parade of circus performers. (Left, Gerald L. Treadway.)

At one point, local residents took part in a minstrel show as part of a community event. The photographs on this page show two of the performers. Minstrel shows were uniquely American entertainment in the years following the Civil War. They were performed by either white or black performers in blackface and consisted of comic skits, variety acts, dancing, and music. The typical minstrel performance included three acts. The first part consisted of a dance, comedy, and songs. The second part featured a variety of entertainments, and the show concluded with music and comedy.

Many community events revolved around the Parkesburg Fire Company. According to census reports, about 58 percent of the borough's adults are married, and households are larger than most, which is consistent with the family emphasis of Parkesburg. The borough also has a diverse population for Pennsylvania, with several racial groups well represented. Above is a fire department meeting in May 1959 with a presentation being made. The photograph below shows three fire vehicles in front of the department.

Some residents of Parkesburg like to collect memorabilia concerning the borough, including photographs and postcards. The above photograph shows an early street scene. The Hotel Parkesburg sign can be seen to the right. A dog is walking in the street on the left side of the road. The photograph below is an aerial view of Parkesburg. (Bill Wilde.)

The smokestacks of the Parkesburg Iron Company and the railroad tracks can be seen in the photograph above. The borough's defining feature has been described as the east–west rail line that bisects it. At one time, it was the main line of the Pennsylvania Railroad. The Parkesburg stop on the rail line was also used at one time as a repair station. The image below shows the Methodist church, which is located on Main Street. (Bill Wilde.)

The two early street scenes of Parkesburg show the borough's business district in the late 19th and early 20th century. The borough charged and grew during those years. Above, horse-drawn wagons are on both sides of the street. A man in a hat is about to enter a store to the left. The postcard image below shows a sign indicating the location of the Parkesburg Army and Navy store on Main Street looking west from Gay Street. (Bill Wilde.)

MAIN STREET LOOKING WEST FROM GAY STREET, PARKESBURG, PENNA.

Rapid changes took place in Parkesburg and throughout the county from 1890 to 1910. Some of those changes are clear in the photographs on this page. The above photograph shows commerce geared to the era of the horse. A sign for horseshoe work is seen in the image, and three men are seen standing near a horse carriage. The image below shows two cars on Main Street and men near a borough barbershop. The scene is looking west from West Street in Parkesburg. (Bill Wilde.)

The above photograph looks west on Main Street. In the lower portion of the photograph, a watering fountain can be seen, which was first installed for horses. Horses were instrumental in the early commerce of Parkesburg. As automobiles became popular, horses became less important. One of the town's churches can be seen on the hill to the right. The image below shows the soldiers' monument on Main Street. A large crowd turned out for the dedication of the monument after World War I. (Bill Wilde.)

The residents of Parkesburg held a number of celebrations for various events over the years. Preparations for one celebration are underway in the photograph at left. A number of flags are shown hung over a borough street. Many of the buildings have also been decorated. The crowds have not yet arrived. The photograph below shows a horse-drawn wagon near the street and an empty wagon to the left. No other activity is seen on the streets. (Bill Wilde.)

The Parkesburg Fire Company has been protecting the citizens of the borough for more than a century. Chester County Court granted a charter to the Parkesburg Hose Company No. 1 on June 11, 1894, but the fire company was organized in 1872, the same year Parkesburg became a borough. Above, a fireman helps fight a blaze. He has on his boots and other gear. The truck's hoses are deployed. The photograph below is a view of one of the borough's churches. (Bill Wilde.)

Above, a young Parkesburg resident takes time out of a busy day to pose for the camera. He is seen on a borough street sitting on a pile of wood. One of Parkesburg's homes can be seen in the background. The business district of Parkesburg is seen below in a photograph of Gay Street looking north. The two main business streets of Parkesburg are First Avenue and Main Street, and they run east and west. (Bill Wilde.)

GAY STREET, LOOKING NORTH, PARKESBURG, PA.

A dominating landmark in Parkesburg for years was the Parkesburg Iron Company. Above is a view of the plant from the hill to the north. The company was organized and incorporated with a capital of $125,000 in 1882. The officers were Horace A. Beale, president; William H. Gibbons, vice president; Amos Michener, secretary; Samuel R. Parke, treasurer; and A. J. Williams, general manager. These persons remained in their respective places until the fall of 1897, when Beale died. The photograph below is of the railroad and station. (Bill Wilde.)

The Parkesburg Iron Company produced quality railroad equipment and other products for a number of years. The above photograph shows workers in the plant. Their days were long and the work was hard. Below is a postcard of the company and the railroad tracks running to the complex. The product of the mills included boiler tube and iron skelp, with the annual output at one time being 20,000 tons. The company had three mill buildings, one forge building, three charcoal houses, two scrap houses, a machine shop, two trimming houses, and other buildings. (Bill Wilde.)

Parkesburg developed, with the help of the iron company, into a thriving borough. The above photograph shows how the borough has developed. The photograph below shows work being completed at the Parkesburg Iron Company. The iron company greatly expanded its operation during its years of operation. (Bill Wilde.)

The Parkesburg Free Library is one of the partners in this book, and it is an integral part of the community, offering valuable services to the residents of the borough. The above photograph shows a gathering of residents inspecting a fire truck. The fire department was central to many community celebrations. The photograph below shows a piece of equipment from the experimental laboratory of radio station WQAA, 3ZO and 301 in Parkesburg.

The experimental laboratory of radio station WQAA, 3ZO and 301 was a mobile radio unit. The station is shown above. The small building is mounted on the back of a truck, and entrance to the station is gained by climbing a ladder in back. The station needed a number of pieces of equipment to operate. The photograph at right shows one of those necessary elements. The experimental radio station operated in the early part of the 20th century.

The small, experimental radio station needed wires and lines to transmit. The above photograph shows lines running between two large poles in a field near the center of the Parkesburg business district. Several homes and trees can be seen in the background. The small radio station did not have a lot of room, and the inside was cramped because of the needed equipment. Some of the equipment is show below. Parkesburg was one of the first communities in the area to have its own radio station.

Parkesburg has a number of historic buildings. The above photograph shows the home once belonging to the Parke family. John G. Parke was a noted politician from the prominent family. Relative Gen. John G. Parke served during the Civil War and played a prominent role in many campaigns. Not all the buildings were as well preserved. The photograph below shows the Parkesburg Academy on Chapel Avenue as seen in 1972.

Many residents have volunteered several hours to worthwhile civic organizations. The volunteers make Parkesburg a great place to live. Chester County has been voted one of the most desirable places to work and live in the nation. The above photograph shows a plaque honoring T. Marshall Bireley, one of the volunteer members of the Parkesburg Fire Company. The photograph below shows the Parke estate.

Members of the Parkesburg Fire Company are always ready to protect the town's residents and property against the threat of fire. The above photograph shows two members of the department sitting in a vehicle that dates from the early part of the 20th century. The location appears to be near the Parkesburg Iron Company. The photograph below shows a local fire. Despite precautions and modern-day rules and regulations, fires can occur. The house is engulfed in flames. The interior can be clearly seen.

Some traditions never change, but public habits do. The above photograph is of a banquet held in Parkesburg. Many organizations hold annual dinners to honor different members for their work during the year. This Parkesburg Fire Company dinner was held in April 1970. Notice the two men at the bottom left of the photograph smoking pipes. The habit of smoking at public functions has ceased to exist. The photograph below shows a volunteer fireman making sure a field fire has been extinguished. Brush fires pose a danger in the region.

The above photograph shows three vehicles from the Parkesburg Fire Company and members of the department appearing relaxed and getting ready for a public event. This photograph could have originally been from a private collection, as the man standing before the middle vehicle is circled. No identifications are given. The location appears to be near the town's iron company. The photograph at right shows the catcher for one of the semiprofessional baseball teams fielded by the Parkesburg Iron Company during the early 20th century.

One of Parkesburg's most notable old homes was the Morris-Hall property on South Gay Street. The 10-acre estate had a sunken garden and at one time was a resort. The tag line for the promotion of the resort was "In Search of Zest–Come for a Rest." The above photograph shows the front of an advertising booklet for the resort. The brochure had a photograph of the gardens and others of bedrooms, the living room, and the dining room. The photograph below shows another notable landmark of Parkesburg, the fire station. It is shown in winter with the last of a snowstorm on the front lawn.

The gardens at the Morris-Hall property on South Gay Street were just one of the many Parkesburg attractions during the early part of the 20th century. The image below is from the advertising brochure that pinpoints Parkesburg between Lancaster and Philadelphia. Parkesburg is 21 miles east of Lancaster and 40 miles west of Philadelphia. It has a historic past built by business, government leaders, and the hard work of its citizens.

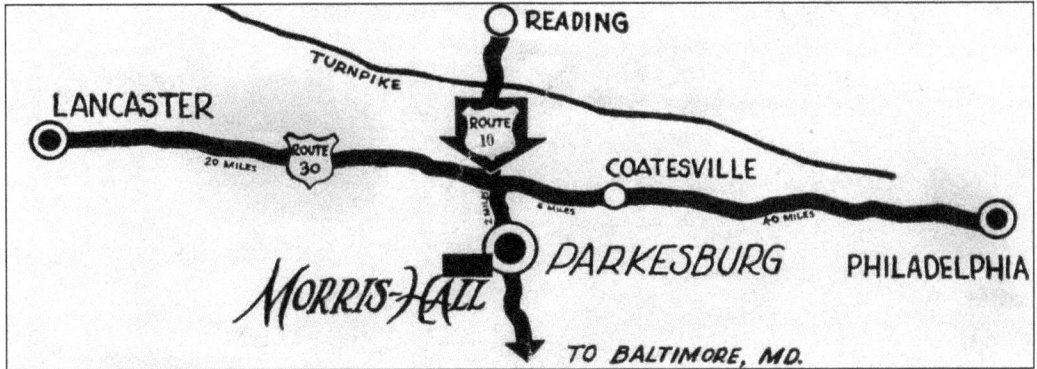

Visit us at
arcadiapublishing.com

www.ingramcontent.com/pod-product-compliance
Lightning Source LLC
Chambersburg PA
CBHW050713110426
42813CB00007B/2172